Ponies and Horses

FIRST EDITION
Series Editor Deborah Lock; **US Editor** John Searcy;
Project Art Editor Mary Sandberg; **Production Editor** Siu Yin Chan; **Production** Claire Pearson;
Jacket Designer Mary Sandberg; **Reading Consultant** Linda Gambrell, PhD

THIS EDITION
Editorial Management by Oriel Square
Produced for DK by WonderLab Group LLC
Jennifer Emmett, Erica Green, Kate Hale, *Founders*

Editors Grace Hill Smith, Libby Romero, Michaela Weglinski;
Photography Editors Kelley Miller, Annette Kiesow, Nicole DiMella;
Managing Editor Rachel Houghton; **Designers** Project Design Company;
Researcher Michelle Harris; **Copy Editor** Lori Merritt; **Indexer** Connie Binder;
Proofreader Larry Shea; **Reading Specialist** Dr. Jennifer Albro; **Curriculum Specialist** Elaine Larson

Published in the United States by DK Publishing
1745 Broadway, 20th Floor, New York, NY 10019

Copyright © 2023 Dorling Kindersley Limited
DK, a Division of Penguin Random House LLC
23 24 25 26 10 9 8 7 6 5 4 3
004–333454–Mar/2023

A catalog record for this book
is available from the Library of Congress.
HC ISBN: 978-0-7440-6789-7
PB ISBN: 978-0-7440-6790-3

DK books are available at special discounts when purchased
in bulk for sales promotions, premiums, fundraising, or
educational use. For details, contact: DK Publishing Special Markets,
1745 Broadway, 20th Floor, New York, NY 10019
SpecialSales@dk.com

Printed and bound in China

The publisher would like to thank the following for their kind permission to reproduce their images:
a=above; c=center; b=below; l=left; r=right; t=top; b/g=background

Alamy: Peter Llewellyn 17; **Corbis:** Walter Bieri / EPA 22; **Dreamstime.com:** Warangkana Charuyodhin 4-5,
Elena Titarenco 12, 13; **DK Images:** Miss. H Houlden ac, Stephen Oliver 2t, 8c; **FLPA:** Gerard Lacz 18–19; **Getty Images:**
Gallo Images / Travel Ink 6-7b; **Getty Images / iStock:** NiKita Filippov 20-21; **Masterfile:** R. Ian Lloyd 26-27; **Shutterstock:**
Picture Partners 9, Kondrashov Mlkhail Evgenevich 16, Dennis Donohue 24-25; **SuperStock:** Age Fotostock 28-29

Cover images: *Front:* **123RF.com:** Olga Itina b; **Shutterstock:** Macrovector tr, br, Vector_Up;
Back: **Shutterstock:** Macrovector tl, cra, bl

All other images © Dorling Kindersley Limited

For the curious
www.dk.com

Ponies and Horses

Fiona Lock

Contents

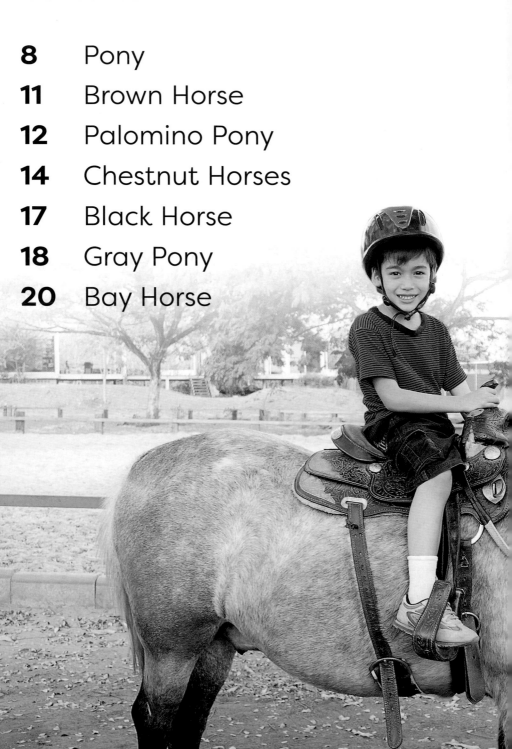

Welcome to
the stable yard.
This is where the horses
eat and drink.

hay

Pony

The pony has to be brushed and washed.

brush

grooming kit

Brown Horse

The brown horse has horseshoes fitted to its hooves.

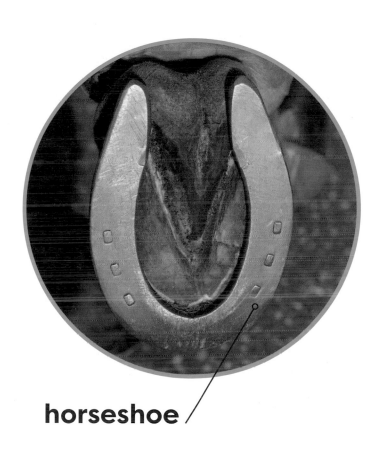

horseshoe

Palomino Pony

The rider puts a saddle on the palomino pony.

palomino pony
[pal-uh-MEE-no]

saddle

Chestnut Horses

The chestnut horses go for a walk wearing bridles. The riders wear riding hats.

riding hat

bridle

Black Horse

The black horse at the horse show performs tricks for people.

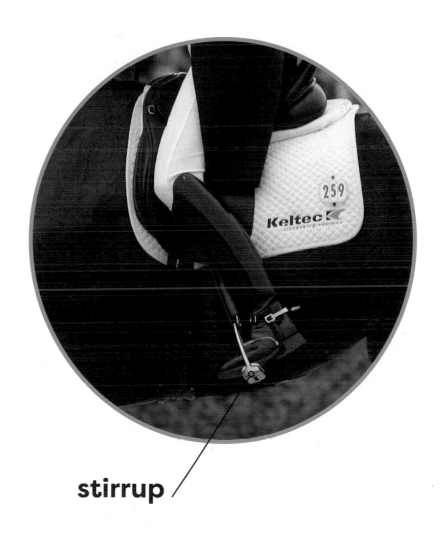

stirrup

Gray Pony

The rider tells
the gray pony to trot
and then to canter.

rider

Bay Horse

The reddish-brown bay horse jumps over the fence.

fence

Dancing Horses

The dancing horses jump and leap.

hooves

Racehorses

The racehorses race around the track.

Who will win?

jockey

track

Ranch Horses

Ranchers ride
ranch horses to
round up the cattle.

rancher

cattle

Wild Horses

The wild horses gallop across a river.

Glossary

brush
a tool for brushing the hair of a horse

fence
a row of bars for a horse to jump over

hooves
the feet of a horse

riding hat
a hard hat that a rider wears

saddle
a seat for a rider that is tied onto a horse's back

Index

Quiz

Answer the questions to see what you have learned. Check your answers with an adult.

1. What is fitted to a horse's hooves?

2. What do a rider and horse do at a horse show?

3. What is the rider of a racehorse called?

4. What do ranchers and ranch horses do?

5. What would you like to do if you had your own horse? How would you take care of your horse?

1. Horseshoes 2. Perform tricks for people 3. A jockey
4. Round up cattle 5. Answers will vary